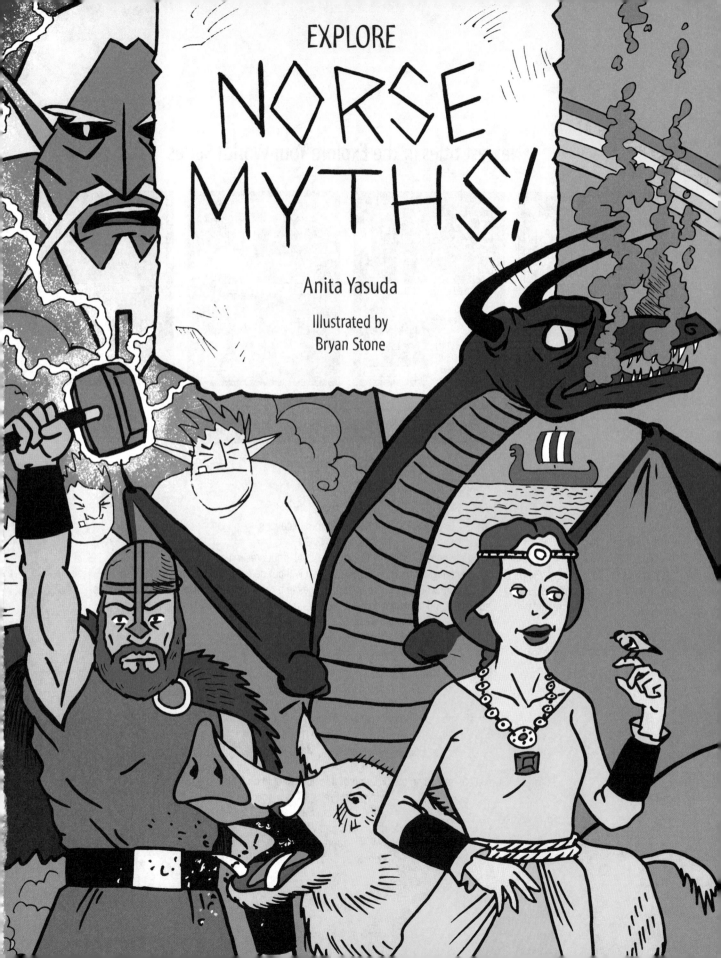

EXPLORE

NORSE MYTHS!

Anita Yasuda

Illustrated by
Bryan Stone

Newest titles in the **Explore Your World!** Series

Check out more titles at www.nomadpress.net

Nomad Press
A division of Nomad Communications
10 9 8 7 6 5 4 3 2 1

This book was manufactured by Marquis Book Printing,
Montmagny, Québec, Canada
November 2015, Job #115327

ISBN Softcover: 978-1-61930-320-1
ISBN Hardcover: 978-1-61930-316-4

Illustrations by Bryan Stone
Educational Consultant, Marla Conn

Questions regarding the ordering of this book should be addressed to
Nomad Press
2456 Christian St.
White River Junction, VT 05001
www.nomadpress.net
Printed in Canada.

CONTENTS

Interested in primary sources? Look for this icon.

Use a smartphone or tablet app to scan the QR code and explore more about Norse myths! You can find a list of URLs on the Resources page.

If the QR code doesn't work, try searching the Internet with the Keyword Prompts to find other helpful sources.

KEYWORD PROMPTS

Norse mythology

TIMELINE

793: Vikings attack the monastery of Lindisfarne located on England's eastern coast, beginning the Viking Age.

958: Harald Blataud becomes king of Denmark.

GREENLAND

ICELAND

ATLANTIC OCEAN

876: Vikings establish permanent settlements in England.

NORTH AMERICA

794: Vikings launch attacks in northern England, now called Scotland.

982: Erik the Red, after being banished from Iceland, finds Greenland.

874: Norsemen successfully settle in Iceland.

986: Erik the Red leads the first settlers to Greenland.

845: Vikings led by Ragnar Lodbrok attack Paris and are later paid a ransom of 7,000 pounds of silver to leave.

870: Norwegian Floki Vilgerdarson discovers Iceland.

992: Leif Erikson, the son of Erik the Red, becomes the first European to reach North America.

866: A Viking army captures York, England.

SOUTH AMERICA

NORWAY
SWEDEN
DENMARK
ENGLAND
BALTIC SEA
EUROPE
AFRICA
ASIA

1066: King Harald of Norway leads an army to invade England but is defeated. The Viking Age ends.

2014: A 1,000-year-old Viking hoard of gold and silver is discovered in Scotland.

1903: The Oseberg Viking ship burial is discovered.

2013: Two Danish teens find 60 rare Norse coins.

1016: Cnut the Great, son of Sweyn Forkbeard, reconquers England.

1960: The Viking colony at L'Anse aux Meadows is discovered by archaeologists Helge Ingstad and Anne Stine Ingstad.

2012: Archaeologists in northern Germany discover what may be the fabled Viking town of Sliasthorp, referred to in texts as the center of power for the first Scandinavian kings.

1013: King Sweyn Forkbeard of Denmark conquers England.

1997: The largest Viking boat ever discovered is found by workers in Denmark's Roskilde Fjord.

v

Do you like stories of heroes, villains, and mystical lands teeming with magical characters? Welcome to the once-upon-a-time land of fire and ice! This is the world of **Norse myths**, which are ancient stories from northern Europe. Why did the Norse people create these myths? What do they tell us about the real Norse people?

In this book, you'll discover poets called **skalds**, raiders called **Vikings**, warriors called **berserkers**, and a terrific cast of different characters.

Words 2 Know

Norse: the people of ancient Norway, Sweden, Denmark, and Iceland.

myth: a traditional story that expresses the beliefs and values of a group of people.

skald: a professional Norse poet.

Vikings: people from Scandinavia who raided coastal towns in Europe between the eighth and tenth centuries.

berserker: a ferocious, uncontrollable fighter.

1

You'll read myths and **legends** about heroes and villains, including Odin, Thor, Loki, and the giant Surtur. But first, let's meet the people of Scandinavia.

◇◇◇◇◇ THE NORSE PEOPLE ◇◇◇◇◇

Scandinavia is in Northern Europe and includes Norway, Sweden, and Denmark. Long ago, the people who lived there were members of many different **tribes** that shared the same language and gods.

DID YOU KNOW?

The incredible ships of the Vikings allowed them to reach North America from ancient Scandinavia. They arrived there five centuries before Christopher Columbus!

From the eighth to the twelfth centuries, the people of Scandinavia were called Norsemen. This means *Men of the North*. They were also called Vikings. Vikings carried out surprise raids on coastal towns. They took as much treasure as they could carry and then sailed away—fast!

2

No one knows the exact meaning of the word *Viking*. In **Old English**, Viking, or *wicing*, means *pirate*. In **Old Norse**, the word *vik* means *bay*. It also means a place in Norway called Viken, where Viking ships sailed from. If a man went on a raid, people said that he had "*gone Viking*."

Most Norsemen hunted and fished, grew **crops**, and raised **livestock**. They were also skilled ship builders. Their ships were the best the world had ever seen. Vikings gave their ships names, such as *Snake of the Sea*.

Norsemen used their ships to push beyond their own region of Scandinavia to explore and trade. Their vast trade network stretched from central Asia to the Arctic. Their adventurous spirit even brought them to North America, more than 3,000 miles away!

The Norse settled in these new lands. They brought their families with them and built farms. Some people worked as craftsmen and others as traders.

Old English: a language spoken in England between the fifth and eleventh centuries.

Old Norse: a language spoken during the Viking Age.

crops: plants grown for food and other uses.

livestock: animals raised for food and other uses.

Words 2 Know

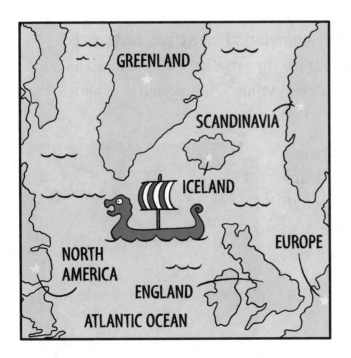

GREENLAND

SCANDINAVIA

ICELAND

NORTH AMERICA

EUROPE

ENGLAND

ATLANTIC OCEAN

KEYWORD PROMPTS

merriam-webster 🔍

PS **Many of the names in this book are hard to say, but you can hear them spoken online.** Go to Merriam-Webster.com, search for the word, and press the 🔊 symbol next to your word to hear it spoken.

◇◇◇◇◇◇◇◇ MYTHS FROM THE NORSE ◇◇◇◇◇◇◇◇

Do you like good stories? The Norse told exciting stories about gods and heroes. Their stories had dramatic beginnings, twists and turns, and surprise endings.

Norse **mythology** helped people understand their world. When the sky thundered or the earth trembled, people blamed it on the gods. Even the mountains and oceans and rivers of their homeland had **supernatural** beginnings in myths. Stories also described what happened when people died.

Myths are fictional, which means they are not true, but we can learn about the lives of the Norse through the stories they told. There are also many different versions of the myths, which can be confusing.

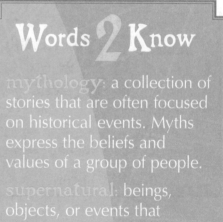

Words 2 Know

mythology: a collection of stories that are often focused on historical events. Myths express the beliefs and values of a group of people.

supernatural: beings, objects, or events that cannot be explained.

Norse gods were like people. They could be angry, sad, jealous, or in love. Norse gods did not live forever. Some Norse gods were wise, such as Odin, the father of the gods. He was the powerful ruler of the gods, usually shown wearing a wide-brimmed hat and carrying a spear.

Others gods, such as Thor, relied on strength. Thor never hesitated to use his magical hammer to defeat the enemies of the gods, including the frost giants.

MEDALS FROM THE PAST

Gold medals called **bracteates** are some of the earliest evidence of Norse myths. They were made in the fifth and sixth centuries and discovered by **archaeologists**. One medal found in Sweden shows a god named Tyr battling the gigantic wolf Fenrir. In the story, the gods learn that Fenrir will help end the world. They decide to try to tie Fenrir up with a chain.

Fenrir is so strong that the chain breaks easily. Dwarfs then fashion a magical chain and the gods trick Fenrir into proving his strength once more. Fenrir agrees, but only if a god puts an arm in his mouth. Courageous Tyr volunteers, but when Fenrir is unable to break free, he bites off Tyr's arm!

Words 2 Know

bracteate: a thin metal disc with an engraved image that could be worn around the neck.

archaeologist: a person who studies ancient people through the objects they left behind.

5

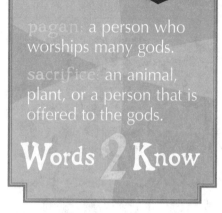
There were also human heroes in Norse myths, such as Prince Sigurd. Armed with a magical sword, Prince Sigurd was able to slay a dragon.

The gods and other supernatural creatures in the Norse myths were actually described in earlier stories. These were told by tribes in Germany and other parts of Europe. The Norse added their own details to these stories through hundreds of years.

OLD NORSE RELIGION

The Norse were **pagans**. We know they worshiped many gods instead of just one. But, because they didn't write history books, very little is known about how the Norse worshiped their gods.

In the eleventh century, a traveler named Adam of Bremen wrote about a large pagan temple in Uppsala, now called Gamla Uppsala, in Sweden. Adam wrote that it looked like a theater with hills all around it. From its roof hung an impressive gold chain that could be seen from far away. Inside the temple stood statues of Odin, Thor, and Freya. He also described **sacrifices** of men and animals.

Gamla Uppsala existed before photography, but you can see a woodcut made in 1555. What do you notice about the temple?

KEYWORD PROMPTS

Gamla Uppsala 🔍

After the Norse became Christian, around 1,000 years ago, pagan temples were burned down. In the twelfth century, King Inge replaced Gamla Uppsala with a Christian church. This was a symbol to tell his subjects that the old gods were gone.

TWO HEAVENLY FAMILIES

There were two families of Norse gods. The Aesir, such as Thor, were warrior gods who were courageous and strong. They controlled the forces in the sky, including thunder. The Vanir gods, including Frey, were gentle. They cared for the earth and the sea.

One myth tells of a time when the two sides did not get along. After a war that neither side could win, they agreed to live in peace. As part of this agreement, the Vanir sent Njord and his children, the twins Frey and Freya, to the Aesir. The Aesir sent Odin's brother Hoenir and a wise god called Mimir to the Vanir. Why might blending the families help keep the peace?

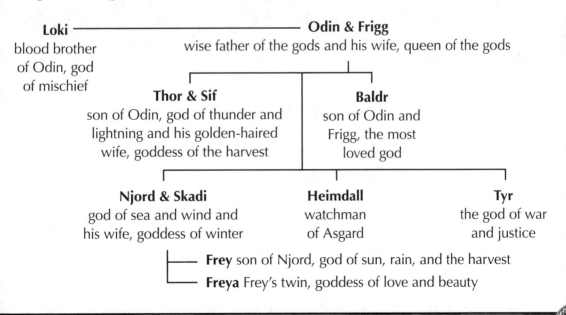

Loki ──────────── **Odin & Frigg**
blood brother of Odin, god of mischief — wise father of the gods and his wife, queen of the gods

Thor & Sif
son of Odin, god of thunder and lightning and his golden-haired wife, goddess of the harvest

Baldr
son of Odin and Frigg, the most loved god

Njord & Skadi
god of sea and wind and his wife, goddess of winter

Heimdall
watchman of Asgard

Tyr
the god of war and justice

Frey son of Njord, god of sun, rain, and the harvest
Freya Frey's twin, goddess of love and beauty

medieval: the period of European history between the fall of the Roman Empire and the Renaissance, from about 350 to about 1450.

saga: a long poem.

fates: powers that are believed to control what happens in the future.

Words 2 Know

THE EDDAS

The *Poetic Edda* and the *Prose Edda* are **medieval** manuscripts from Iceland. They are our main sources of information about Norse myths. The *Poetic Edda* is a collection of 38 ancient Norse stories, called **sagas**, written by many different authors. They were part of a manuscript named the *Codex Regius*, which means *king's manuscript*.

An Icelandic poet, politician, and historian called Snorri Sturluson used these stories to write the *Prose Edda,* or *Younger Edda*. Sturluson added many details to the stories from sources that are no longer available. He hoped that other poets would read his work and use it as a guide.

You can read the *Prose Edda* here. Is the language easy to read? Does it sound different from the stories we read today?

KEYWORD PROMPTS

Prose Edda Translation 🔍

NINE WORLDS

The Norse believed that there were nine worlds divided into three different levels. A magnificent elm tree called Yggdrasil grew through the middle. An eagle sat at the top of the tree and a snake gnawed on the roots below. Three **fates** spun yarn around the tree and cared for it. The yarn stood for the path a person's life would take.

Then

Once, Vikings spoke a language called Old Norse.

NOW

The main languages in Scandinavia are Swedish, Norwegian, Danish, and Finnish. People who speak Swedish, Norwegian, and Danish are able to understand each other because the languages are similar.

The Norse believed that their paths were decided by the fates, which represented present, past, and future.

Humans lived in the center level, in Midgard, or Middle Earth. The giants of Jotunheim and the dwarfs of Nidavellir lived there too. The gods lived at the top in Asgard and Vanaheim, as did the Light Elves of Alfheim. A rainbow bridge of fire, air, and water called Bifröst joined Middle Earth to Asgard.

It was Heimdall's job to guard the bridge from frost giants, who were always threatening to destroy Asgard. Between Middle Earth and the lowest tier was Svartalfheim, Land of the Dark Elves.

HOW DID VIKINGS SEND MESSAGES?

JUST FOR LAUGHS

With Norse code!

The dead who had not died in battle lived in Niflheim, and Hel was at the bottom. No one wanted to go to this dark region, not even the gods!

CE: put after a date, CE stands for Common Era and counts up from zero. BCE stands for Before Common Era and counts down to zero. These non-religious terms correspond to BC and AD. This book was published in 2015 CE.

Words 2 Know

In *Explore Norse Myths!*, you'll explore the fascinating geography, technology, language, and arts of the Viking Age. This exciting time, from about 700 to 1000 CE, was when the Norse people became great explorers and traders. Let's join them on a legendary journey!

GOOD STUDY PRACTICES

Every good mythologist keeps a study journal! Choose a notebook to use as your study journal. As you learn about Norse myths, use your study journal to keep track of your observations and ideas. A scientific method worksheet helps organize experiments.

Each chapter of this book begins with an essential question to help guide your exploration of Norse myths.

? ESSENTIAL QUESTION

Do you think the Vikings had a choice in how they behaved?

Keep the question in your mind as you read the chapter. At the end of each chapter, use your study journal to record your thoughts and answers.

Question: What are we trying to find out? What problem are we trying to solve?

Research: What do other people think?

Hypothesis/Prediction: What do we think the answer will be?

Equipment: What supplies are we using?

Method: What procedure are we following?

Results: What happened and why?

ACTIVITY

MAKE BRACTEATES

Norse craftsmen hammered images onto thin metal discs called bracteates. Archaeologists have found bracteates with images from Norse myths. In this activity, you are going to make your own.

1 Trace around the bottle cap on your paper. Make as many circles as you like.

2 Draw a design on the circle. Make it simple, because later you will be going over it with glue. Some ideas for designs are Thor's hammer or Odin's spear. Cut the circles out.

3 Go over the design with the glue pen, leaving a nice thick line.

4 Once your bracteates have dried, spread out your newsprint. Pour the paint onto the paper plate and paint your bracteates.

5 When your bracteates are dry, you can turn them into pendants. Take a twist tie and peel off the paper. Fold the tie in half and twist it to make a loop. Secure one to each bracteate with a piece of tape and thread yarn through the loop.

SUPPLIES

* bottle cap or similarly sized round object
* pencil
* heavy paper from recycled greeting cards
* scissors
* glue pen
* newsprint
* gold paint
* paper plate
* paintbrush
* twist ties
* tape
* yarn

ACTIVITY

NINE WORLD WOODCUT

The Norse believed the universe was split into nine worlds, with a giant elm tree in the middle. In this activity, you'll make a woodcut for each world.

1 Do some brainstorming in your study journal about what to draw to represent the nine worlds. Are you going to draw different gods? An eagle, snake, or squirrel? What images best represent the nine worlds?

2 Cut the edges off the trays and then cut them into different sizes depending on what you plan to draw.

3 Push the tip of the pen into the foam to draw. Add dots or other shapes to make your picture more interesting. Try to fill the space. Repeat this step until you have an image for all nine worlds.

4 Dip your sponge into the paint and cover your design. Places without paint will appear white.

5 Press your design firmly onto the paper. Apply more paint if the design is unclear. If you want more white showing, use toothpicks to scrape off some paint.

6 You can make individual pictures or press the block onto one large sheet of paper. Let your prints dry before hanging them.

SUPPLIES

* 4–6 foam trays (clean and dry)
* scissors
* pen
* black acrylic paint
* sponge
* heavy white paper from leftover greeting cards
* toothpicks

CHAPTER 1
A GIANT UNIVERSE

It was a mystery to the Norse why thunder rumbled across the sky. The change of the seasons from winter to spring to summer to fall seemed magical. Even the land the Norse lived on and the vast seas they sailed across were puzzles.

Today, people turn to science to explain the world. But long ago, people used myths to explain **natural phenomena** such as thunder, mountains, islands, **glaciers**, **fjords**, and changing seasons.

? ESSENTIAL QUESTION

Why did the Norse explain their world through myths?

Words 2 Know

natural phenomenon: an event, such as a thunderstorm or an earthquake, that is created by nature, not by people.

fjord: a long, narrow inlet of the sea, usually with steep cliffs on both sides.

glacier: a huge mass of ice and snow.

13

Words 2 Know

Look at the map at the beginning of the book. You can see that much of Scandinavia is bordered by the Atlantic Ocean and the Baltic Sea. The Norse knew that **tides** affected their land in cycles, but they didn't know how or why. They turned to myths to explain.

In Norse myth, Aegir, the god of the sea, lived in a dazzling palace full of treasure from sunken ships. Aegir was a great host who brewed **mead**, in a cauldron 5 miles deep, for the gods to drink. Thor was said to have once taken such a long drink from the ocean, thinking it was mead, that he caused the first tides. Do you know what really causes the tides?

Denmark is made of more than 400 islands. An ancient story tells how the goddess Gefion created Denmark's largest island, Zealand. Wanting a piece of land, the goddess made a mischievous plan and traveled to the court of a mythical Swedish king. The king agreed to give her as much land as she could plow during one day and night using only four oxen.

WHERE DID LITTLE VIKINGS GO WHEN THEY FELT SICK?

JUST FOR LAUGHS

The School *Norse!*

Gefion, who was married to a giant, changed her four huge sons into bulls. The bulls were so strong that they ripped the land from Sweden! Today, Gefion is honored with a fountain on the harborfront in Copenhagen, Denmark's capital.

◈◈ GIANTS AND TROLLS ◈◈

At the beginning of the eighth century, people lived in small farming villages along the coasts, rivers, and lakes of Scandinavia. Much of the rest of the land was too rocky and mountainous to farm. In fact, Scandinavia has more than 130 mountains, many more than 6,500 feet tall! No wonder people imagined giants living there.

MEET THE GODS

THOR

Thor was Odin's incredibly strong son. He was the god of thunder who traveled across the sky in a chariot pulled by two goats. Thor was huge and had red hair. Some stories said that fiery embers flew from his hair when he was angry.

PS Vikings wore amulets shaped like Thor's hammer to bring them luck.

KEYWORD PROMPTS

Thor's hammer amulet 🔍

Many of the stories in the Eddas tell of unusual creatures, such as a giant who had two children born in the form of wolves. Two other children were born to a man on Middle Earth. He called them Sun and Moon.

The man's boldness angered the gods, so they stole the children and placed them in the sky. The monstrous wolf children, named Skoll and Hati, leaped into the heavens where they began to chase forever after Sun and Moon, hoping to return the world to darkness. What natural phenomenon does this myth explain?

Then

The Vikings made ice skates from horse or cow bones that they tied to the bottom of their shoes with leather. They used a long pole to push themselves across the ice because bone skates were slow. Skaters might have reached speeds of 2.5 miles per hour (mph).

NOW

Ice skates are made with strong metal blades and molded plastic or leather boots. Speed skaters are so fast that they can reach speeds of 40 mph!

ICE AND FIRE

Thousands of years ago, glaciers carved U-shaped valleys through the mountains of Scandinavia. These deep valleys, called fjords, are breathtakingly beautiful.

If you were a Norse farmer living in one part of Norway, how would you trade with farmers and craftsmen in other parts of the region? You probably sailed down a fjord.

A fjord in Norway called the Naeroyfjord is named for the god Njord. The Naeroyfjord was an important transportation route. It was easier to sail down fjords than it was to hike across steep mountain paths.

A Norse legend tells of magical creatures using Mount Beitelen to carve the Naeroyfjord. Beitel is a word from the Old Norse language meaning *chisel*. The Norse didn't have knowledge of glaciers and ice ages. It made sense to them that a giant used a mountain to carve a deep channel in the earth.

DID YOU KNOW?

Many places are connected to myths. Iceland's Ásbyrgi canyon is a horseshoe-shaped canyon with stone walls that soar up to 328 feet in height. It is said that Sleipnir, Odin's horse, created it when they were riding one day.

Norse myths are also full of fiery lands. In reality, Iceland, which the Norse settled, has more than 150 volcanoes! Stories in the *Eddas* tell of the fire giant Surtur, who ruled a land of raging lava and flame. Sounds like Iceland, doesn't it?

Fire and ice play important roles in the Norse creation myth. You can read it on the next page.

THE NORSE CREATION MYTH

In the beginning, there was no earth, sea, or air. There was only a huge, dark gap dividing the frozen mist of Niflheim and the fire of Muspelheim. Showers of sparks from Muspelheim hissed and spluttered as they fell upon Niflheim. Slowly, the ice of Niflheim melted to reveal the frost giant Ymir.

When Ymir rose, a giant and a giantess fell from under his great arms. A six-headed son popped out from under his feet. The ice continued to melt until a cow named Andhumla emerged. She provided the hungry giants with rivers of milk. Andhumla needed food too, so she began to lick the salt off the ice. She licked until the first god, Buri, appeared. Buri had a son called Bor.

Bor married a giantess and they had three powerful sons, Odin, Hoenir, and Lothur. The sons, believing that Ymir made the universe too cold, used Ymir's body to build the world. His flesh became the soil, his bones became the mountains, and his blood became the oceans. The gods raised his skull up to create the sky.

Lastly, Ymir's eyebrows became a wall around Middle Earth to keep the frost giants out. It was here that the first man and woman lived after being made from an elm and ash tree.

THE FOUR SEASONS

What is winter like where you live? Scandinavia is a northern country where hail and freezing rain signal the beginning of the long, dark, icy winter. In the age of Vikings, when ice storms threatened their crops, people might say, "Thor is fighting the frost giants."

After many months of winter, spring comes to Scandinavia. The Norse believed that Frey, the god of sun and rain, brought spring by scattering flowers from his chariot. His **boar** had golden bristles that stood for the brilliant sun. The boar ploughed the earth with its tusks for the farmers to plant their crops. These crops grew into golden fields of grain thanks to Sif, the goddess of the harvest.

Scandinavian summers are short but filled with bright days. Norsemen celebrated the change of seasons with festivals. **Midsummer** was one of the most important celebrations. It was held on the longest day of the year, on the anniversary of the god Baldr's death. Baldr brightened each day with his goodness until he was killed by a spear made from mistletoe. His death stood for the time when the days begin to get shorter again.

boar: a large, pig-like animal.

Midsummer: a holiday celebrating the longest day of the year.

Valkyries: warrior women who carried slain warriors to Odin's hall.

aurora borealis: a natural display of shimmering colors in the night sky, usually only seen in the far north. Also called the northern lights.

Words 2 Know

Did You Know?

When dazzling colored lights lit up the northern skies, people might say, "The Valkyries are riding." Norsemen believed the Valkyries' glittering spears created the aurora borealis.

Words 2 Know

culture: a group of people who share beliefs and a way of life.

As in many other cultures, the Norse explained the seasons with a story in which gods lived part of the year in the cold and the other part in the sun's warmth. You can read this myth below.

Myths helped explain natural phenomenon and they can also show us what was important to people who lived long ago. Let's find out what the Norse cared about.

KNOW YOUR MYTHS

THE MARRIAGE OF SKADI AND NJORD

Skadi, the beautiful daughter of the frost giant Thiazi, stood in Asgard with her bow and arrow at the ready. Skadi had just discovered that the Aesir gods had killed her father. Now, she wanted them to pay.

The gods, who had no quarrel with Skadi, asked her if she would like to marry one of them. Skadi agreed, but when the gods lined up for her to choose, a mysterious mist hid them. Only their feet poked out.

Skadi hoped to choose the handsome Baldr, but instead ended up with the old god of the sea, Njord. Skadi and Njord were opposites. Skadi loved the ice and cold, while Njord preferred the sun and sea. The couple agreed to live nine months in the mountains and the rest of the year by the ocean.

? ESSENTIAL QUESTION

It's time to consider and discuss the Essential Question: Why did the Norse explain their world through myths?

GLACIER MOVEMENT

Glaciers are always on the move. As they move, they scrape and shape the land underneath.

SUPPLIES

* 16-ounce plastic container
* sand or fine gravel
* soil
* water
* freezer
* baking sheet
* cooking spray
* flour
* granola
* study journal

1 Ask an adult to help you cut off the top of the plastic container where it starts to get smaller. Fill the container halfway with fine gravel and sand. Add water to the container until it is three-quarters full. Place your container in the freezer.

2 While your glacier freezes, spray a baking sheet with nonstick cooking spray. Sprinkle flour over the sheet for your land and granola for rocks and soil.

3 Start a scientific method worksheet in your study journal. What is your hypothesis? What will happen to your land when the glacier meets it?

4 Run warm water on the outside of your container to unmold the glacier and place it at one end of the baking sheet. You can either observe your glacier during the next few hours or push it across your landscape.

THINK MORE: How did your results compare to your hypothesis? Try the experiment again and place the baking sheet on a slope. Will this change your results? What did you learn about glaciers?

ACTIVITY

MAP OF SCANDINAVIA

Make a map showing the countries of Sweden, Norway, and Denmark.

SUPPLIES

- Internet access
- printer
- scissors
- mixing bowl
- measuring cups
- 6 cups salt
- 6 cups flour
- 3 cups water
- spoon
- plastic bag
- empty cereal box
- paint (blue, green, brown)
- paintbrushes

1 With an adult's permission, use the Internet to find a **topographical** map of Scandinavia showing the countries of Norway, Sweden, and Denmark. You can print it out to use it for reference.

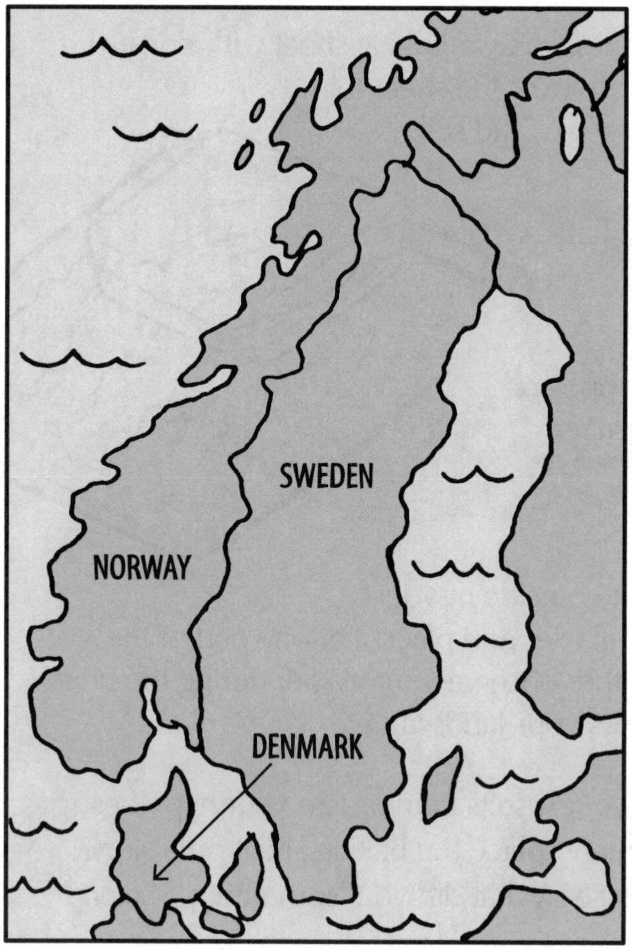

2 Mix the salt, flour, and water in a bowl until they make a dough. Seal one third of the dough in a plastic bag to prevent it from drying out. You will use it later to create topographical features.

Words 2 Know

topographical: having to do with the features of the land, such as mountains.

3 Cut open a cereal box and flatten it for your base. Following the shapes on the map, use the dough to form the three countries. Leave it blank where large bodies of water separate the land.

4 Using the extra dough, add topographical features to your countries, such as major mountain ranges.

5 Paint your map, using blue for water, and brown or green for mountains and farmland.

6 Make flags for each country and label capital cities and major waterways.

THINK MORE: You can also use Google Maps to explore what these countries look like today from space and from the ground. Can you find any old Viking sites? Try looking for Lindholm Høje Stone Ships, Denmark.

LAND, HO!

Scandinavia is a land of islands, volcanoes, and other interesting geography. Using your knowledge of Norse myths, think about how the Norse explained the origin of the landforms around them. Research more myths to find out how people understood the world before they had modern scientific tools and instruments.

SUPPLIES

- mixing bowl
- measuring cups
- 1 cup flour
- ½ cup salt
- large spoon
- water
- food dye (blue, green)
- small loaf pan

MAKE A FJORD

Did you know that Sognefjord is Norway's largest fjord? It is 127 miles long. You are going to create a model of a fjord with play dough. With an adult's permission, research images of fjords online. You can double the play dough recipe if you want more.

1 Stir flour and salt together in the bowl. Then stir in enough water to make a dough that you can handle. If the mixture is too moist, add flour, and if it is too dry, add a little water. Knead the dough to make it soft.

2 Split your dough into three different lumps. Add a drop of blue food dye to some of the dough, knead it in, and spread it in the base of your pan as water.

3 Add a little green food dye to another piece of the dough and knead it in. Mold this around your pan for the fjord's steep slopes.

4 Use any extra dough to make waterfalls, trees, or animals.

THINK MORE: How strong must the natural forces be to create the steep fjord walls? Why were fjords popular harbors for Viking ships?

AURORA BOREALIS COLLAGE

This activity is inspired by the Valkyries' spears. You can make your own auroras with patterned paper cut into different shapes.

1 Color your paper to create a night sky.

2 Create stars on your background with a gold fine-tip marker.

3 From your colorful paper scraps, cut out tiny squares and rectangles. They should be no bigger than a fingertip.

4 From the tinfoil, cut out small triangles to represent the points of the Valkyries spears.

5 Arrange the pieces across the sky. In the example, the pieces are staggered vertically, as the auroras often appear as curtains of color.

6 When you are happy with your picture, secure the pieces with glue and hang your collage on the wall!

Were there really dragons during the time of the Vikings? The kind of dragon that flies and breathes fire is imaginary, but the Norse had dragons that skimmed over the water. Dragon ships!

The dragon ship, or **longboat**, was the Norsemen's best-known ship. Its unique design meant it could be sailed forward or backward without turning around. The ship had a shallow **hull** so it could be sailed right onto a beach. It was also light enough to be carried from one river to another. Some dragon ships had names, such as *Snake of the Sea* or *The Long Serpent*.

? ESSENTIAL QUESTION

Why were the Vikings excellent shipbuilders?

WORDS 2 KNOW

longboat: a large boat powered by oars.

hull: the hollow, lowest part of a ship.

In 1997, a massive Viking ship was discovered near the Viking Ship Museum in Denmark. This ship had room for 100 warriors! Usually, Viking ships fit between 50 and 70 people.

A large square sail made of wool crisscrossed with strips of leather stood in the middle of the ship. Sails could be up to 40 feet tall. That's nearly as high as a four-story building! Some of the sails were solid red, some had stripes, and some had diamond patterns. When there was no wind, men switched to oars to power the ship.

THE LONG SERPENT

One of the most famous ships in history was called *The Long Serpent*. It was built for Olaf Tryggvason, a Norwegian king who ruled from 995 to 1000 CE. The ship had 34 oars on each side.

According to ancient sources, a ship builder called Thorberg thought the finished ship's planks were too thick. Thinking this would make the boat slow, he secretly cut notches into the planks.

King Tryggvason was furious and demanded that Thorberg fix the notches. When he chipped away the notches, though, Thorberg made the planks even thinner, which made the ship very light and fast. King Tryggvason was so pleased he made Thorberg his master builder.

cargo: a load carried on a ship or aircraft.

Words 2 Know

⬦⬦⬦⬦⬦⬦⬦⬦⬦ KNARR SHIPS ⬦⬦⬦⬦⬦⬦⬦⬦⬦

The Norse designed a large ship for trade called the knarr. This ship's hull was shorter and wider than a dragon ship. Traders filled the center with **cargo**, such as wood, iron, fur, leather, and walrus ivory, which made the ship heavy. That is why the knarr relied more on wind than oar power. If the winds were good, a knarr could travel as far as 75 miles in one day.

Like the dragon boat, the knarr's hull was flat. This meant it could be sailed up rivers where the water was very shallow. The knarr was perfect for long voyages because there was lots of room for people, supplies, and livestock.

Then

In 1893, a replica knarr set out from Bergen, Norway, to try to reach North America. It made the 4,000-mile voyage to Newfoundland in only 28 days.

NOW

In 2014, a Viking longship named for a ninth-century Norwegian king, the *Dragon Harald Fairhair*, sailed from Norway to the United Kingdom. The ship was built by hand and took two years to be completed.

⬦⬦⬦⬦⬦⬦⬦ MYTHICAL SHIPS ⬦⬦⬦⬦⬦⬦⬦

Ships were important to the Norse for their survival. It makes sense that the gods they worshiped would have ships, too.

28

Frey's magical ship, *Skidbladnir*, could sail over water. It could fit all the gods and their horses on board. Plus, it could shrink down to the size of a toy. If Frey wanted, he could pop it into his pocket! Loki, the god of mischief, gave the ship and other gifts to the gods after he played a nasty trick on Sif, the goddess of grain. You can read about it below.

KNOW YOUR MYTHS

SIF'S GOLDEN HAIR

On Middle Earth, fields of golden wheat swayed in the wind. Far above the land, Sif, the goddess of grain, lay fast asleep. But she was not alone. Loki had crept up silently to play a trick. With a *snip,* Loki chopped off Sif's hair!

Sif woke to find her hair scattered around her like straw. When Thor discovered what had happened, he flew into a black rage. His eyes glowed red. Lightning danced between the clouds. Thor knew that no one but Loki would dare play such a cruel trick. Thor chased Loki down and made him promise to fix Sif's hair.

Frightened, Loki rushed to find a dwarf who could help him. Loki ran down twisting dark tunnels within the earth, following the rat-a-tat of a hammer until he found a dwarf busy at his fire. Some sources name this dwarf Dvalin. Loki begged him to spin hair for Sif and offered to repay him in the future.

Dvalin worked quickly. When he was done, Loki greedily grabbed the hair. Then, he spied two more wondrous creations and took those too. One was the spear Gungnir, which Loki gave to Odin, and the other was the ship Skidbladnir, which he gave to Frey. As for Sif, she was very pleased with her magical hair. It grew as it had before, but now it outshone even the sun.

29

bow: the front of a ship.

stern: the back of a ship.

artifact: an ancient, man-made object.

Words 2 Know

OSEBERG SHIP

Vikings were buried with their possessions in ships or in graves shaped like ships. They believed they could use their ships and other possessions in the afterlife. In 1906, archaeologists made an amazing find in Oseberg, Norway. They uncovered a ship that was built around 890 CE. The ship was beautifully carved from its **bow** to its **stern**. Two women, one about 80 years old and the other about 50 years old, were buried in the ship's burial chamber, behind the mast, sometime in the thirteenth century. They were buried with buckets of food, sleds, 12 horses, and farm equipment. No one knows who these women were, though they must have been important.

(PS) **You can see pictures of the ship discovered in Oseberg, Norway, and the artifacts found there.**

KEYWORD PROMPTS

Oseberg Viking ship 🔍

◇◇◇◇◇◇◇ SECRETS OF NAVIGATION ◇◇◇◇◇◇◇

The Norse did not have compasses or GPS to guide them across the land and sea. They tried to keep the coast in sight when they sailed. Hills, mountains, and towns all served as visual clues that helped sailors know where they were. Sailors learned to listen for the sound of waves hitting the shore and to track birds, which could lead them back to land.

navigate: to find your way from one place to another.

Words 2 Know

In 860 CE, a man named Floki Vilgerdarson set out for an island he had only heard stories about. Today we know this island as Iceland. Floki released three ravens to help him get there. One flew toward the Faroe Islands, which lie halfway between Norway and Iceland. A second bird stayed near the ship. The third bird flew toward the horizon. Floki followed it until he sighted land. He had made it to Iceland!

Sailors also relied on the stars and sun to help them **navigate**. Polaris, also called the North Star, was the most important star. Polaris is found above the North Pole. Sailors used Polaris to find north, and then they could figure out other directions.

WHAT WAS A VIKINGS FAVORITE STAR?

JUST FOR LAUGHS

The Norse star!

MEET THE GODS

Frigg

Frigg was the goddess of motherhood and the clouds. She could see the future, but she never told people what it was. She worked at her spinning wheel each night, creating special yarn that she gave to women on Middle Earth who she felt deserved it.

During the day, when the stars could not be seen, men used several different instruments to help them navigate. One of these instruments was the bearing circle. This device tracked the position of the sun at sunrise and sunset and helped sailors find their **latitude**.

The sun shadow board was another instrument that sailors used for navigation. This board had a pin in the center and circles carved around it that helped sailors stay at the correct latitude.

To determine a course, navigators placed the board in a bowl of water to keep it level. At noon, a sailor noted where the shadow of the pin fell. A shadow beyond the circle meant the ship was too far north.

Did You Know?

Researchers think it's possible that Vikings used what they called a sun stone to help them navigate on cloudy days. It was made out of a **mineral** called Iceland spar. Because of the way light moves through this mineral, you can tell where the sun is when you look through the stone, even when the sun is blocked.

? ESSENTIAL QUESTION

It's time to consider and discuss the Essential Question:
Why were the Vikings excellent shipbuilders?

VIKING DRAGON SHIP

Design your own dragon ship with a juice box!
Caution: Ask an adult to help you with the scissors.

1 Lay your juice box on a flat surface. With the point of your scissors, cut out a rectangle on the top but be sure to leave one short end attached.

2 Curve this rectangular piece forward and up to form a dragon-shaped bow and tape it in place.

3 Tape the straw down to the center of your box for the mast. Cut out a paper sail. Poke a hole at the top and bottom of the paper sail and push the straw through.

4 Glue buttons for the shields around the outside of the ship. Add a few pebbles to the bottom of your ship for **ballast**.

5 Start a scientific method worksheet. What will happen when you sail your dragon ship in a tub of water?

6 Place your ship on the surface of a tub of water. Blow on the sail and observe how it sails. Record what you see in your journal.

THINK MORE: Based on your observations, adjust the design of your sail. Should it be smaller or larger? What happens if you add or take away ballast?

Words 2 Know

ballast: weight in the bottom of a ship that helps to balance the ship.

SUPPLIES

* Internet access
* large glass jar
* tinfoil
* scissors
* cardboard
* straight pin
* battery-operated tea light

NORSE STARLIGHT

Different cultures have looked at the night sky and seen different shapes. The Norse explained the shapes they saw with myths. The Big Dipper was Thor's chariot. The stars Castor and Pollux in the constellation of Gemini were Thiazi's eyes, which Odin threw into the heavens. The three bright stars of Orion's belt were part of Frigg's spinning wheel. The Little Dipper, which contains the Polaris, was Thor's hammer.

In this activity you are going to make a constellation night-light. With an adult's permission, research these star patterns online: the Big Dipper, Gemini, Orion, and the Little Dipper. Try to find them in the sky at night by using a star chart.

KEYWORD PROMPTS

star chart app 🔍

1 Wrap a piece of foil around the outside of the jar and cut to size. Check to see if this piece fits easily in the jar. It will overlap a little bit.

2 Lay the foil flat on the cardboard.

3 Use the pin to poke holes in the foil in the shapes of the images of the constellations you researched online. All the star patterns do not have to fit on the same sheet. Make several sheets using the same method.

4 Place one of the foil sheets in the jar. Turn on the battery-operated tea light and place it in the jar. **Never use a candle!** Put the lid back on. Turn off the lights and watch as your room is lit with stars!

SUN SHADOW BOARD

Norse sailors used a sun shadow board to stay on course. On land, they tracked the sun and marked its position on the board. At the end of the day, the points were joined to form a circle.

1 Before you begin to observe the sun, start a scientific method worksheet and write down a hypothesis. When do you think the sun's shadow will be the shortest? Why?

2 Secure the stick to the center of the plate with tape. Place the plate in an area where the sun will shine on it all day.

3 Every hour, mark on the plate where the stick's shadow falls.

4 At the end of the day, join the marks to form a curve. This is your East/West line. The point where the curve is nearest the center is your North/South line.

THINK MORE: How did your results compare to your hypothesis? The length of the shadow depends on how high the sun is in the sky. How long was the shadow in the morning? At noon? In the late afternoon? Try this experiment at different times of the year to see if your results are different. Why might your results be different?

CHAPTER 3

EXCITING EXPLORATIONS

Many Norse myths and sagas tell fascinating tales of their journeys across the seas and the challenges they had to overcome to survive. The Norse were great traders and explorers. Trade was the only way the Norse could buy the goods that they couldn't make or find in Scandinavia.

Norse merchants loaded their ships with items for trade, such as walrus ivory, amber, and fur. They set off to buy and sell goods across Europe. Along the way, the Norse explored the world.

? ESSENTIAL QUESTION

How did geography play an important role in Viking history?

◇◇◇◇◇◇◇◇◇◇◇ *TRADING TOWNS* ◇◇◇◇◇◇◇◇◇◇◇

Using the Volga and Dnieper Rivers, Norse traders sailed into Russia, Central Asia, and the Middle East. Others went to North Africa. Towns formed and grew along these trade routes. The biggest Norse trading centers were Birka in Sweden, Kaupang in Norway, and Hedeby on the German-Danish border.

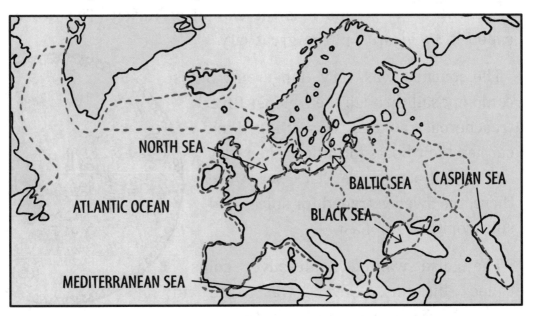

Trading towns were busy places. Merchants and craftsmen, eager to sell their goods, claimed every plot of land. People came to buy goods such as honey or items made of leather or willow.

A peasant might need a **soapstone** pot to cook meals in or a **whetstone** to sharpen tools. Farmers traded surplus wheat or barley or fish. What could you trade two horses for? Maybe a suit of **chain mail**?

soapstone: a type of soft stone that can absorb and give off heat.

whetstone: a stone used for sharpening knives or tools.

chain mail: a type of armor worn by warriors made of interlocking metal links.

37

Byzantine Empire: also called the Eastern Roman Empire, founded by Constantine the Great in 330 CE.

Words 2 Know

◇◇◇◇◇◇◇ THE GREAT CITY ◇◇◇◇◇◇◇

Swedish Vikings traveled more than 1,200 miles for items available only in Constantinople. This city was the capital of a great empire called the **Byzantine Empire**. Today, the city is called Istanbul and it is the capital of Turkey. The Norse called it *Miklagard* or "the great city."

The journey was very dangerous. Ships could not sail through the Dnieper River's treacherous rapids. Crews dragged and carried their boats for miles! Then they had to sail across the Black Sea. Once there, the Swedes traded for spices and silk from the Far East.

They also wanted Arab silver coins called dirhams. Silver was rare in Scandinavia because there were no silver mines. Traders carried scales with them to weigh the coins. A coin's value was based on its weight, because some coins were melted down to make objects such as jewelry.

Did You Know?

Sailors hoped Aegir, god of the sea, would keep the seas calm. No Viking wanted to anger Aegir's wife, Ran. She lured ships onto rocks, netted the men, and dragged treasure to the bottom of the sea. Sailors kept a piece of gold with them at all times to bribe Ran if they needed to.

Do you bring a scale with you when you go to the store? Our money's value is decided by different things, such as how it compares to the value of money in other countries. We no longer have to weigh every penny.

A NEW HOME

From the eighth century, Norse people began to settle outside of Scandinavia. No one knows why. One theory is that the population grew so large that there wasn't enough land for everyone. But there was fertile land nearby in the **British Isles**.

WHY DIDN'T THE VILLAGERS RUN WHEN THEY SAW THE VIKING SHIP?

JUST FOR LAUGHS

They thought it was a friend-ship!

The *Anglo-Saxon Chronicle* is the earliest known history of England written in English. According to the *Anglo-Saxon Chronicle*, around 865 CE, the Norse stopped returning home at the end of each raiding summer. Instead, the "Great Army," as they were called, built winter camps in the British Isles.

At the same time, the Norse army fought and captured many English kingdoms. Realizing that the Vikings planned to stay, Alfred the Great made a deal with the Danish Viking leader, Guthrum, in 878 CE.

39

Alfred gave the Vikings northeastern England. The area became known as Danelaw. For more than half a century, people there lived under Scandinavian law.

Jorvik, which is now called York, was the center of Danelaw. More than 40,000 Viking Age objects, including shoes, brooches, and rings, have been dug up there. Some items came from thousands of miles away, such as a cowrie shell from the Red Sea and an amber axe-head from the Baltic.

DID YOU KNOW?

The word *Anglo-Saxon* refers to the people from Germanic tribes who migrated to the island of Britain.

THE ANGLO-SAXON CHRONICLE

This important historical document was first written in the ninth century in England. Scholars added to the *Anglo-Saxon Chronicle* in later versions, so we now have a record of early history up to 1154.

You can see pictures of a version of the *Anglo-Saxon Chronicle*. Do they look similar to books today?

Read some of the *Anglo-Saxon Chronicle* here. How is the language different from the language in this book? Can you understand it?

KEYWORD PROMPTS

Anglo-Saxon Chronicle 🔍

◇◇◇◇◇◇◇◇◇◇◇ GREAT EXPLORERS ◇◇◇◇◇◇◇◇◇◇◇

Erik the Red's real name was Erik Thorvaldsson. He may have earned his nickname from his hair color, or it may have been his temper, which got him into heaps of trouble. After he fought and killed two people, Erik was told to leave Iceland for three years.

Erik was an adventurous man. He sailed to a place he had only heard of! What he discovered there was a huge, snowy landmass.

After the three years were up, Erik returned to Iceland. He told people about a new "green land" he had discovered. Why did he lie? Have you ever tried to make a miserable experience sound better than it really was? Erik told such good stories that 500 people joined him when he returned to the land he called Greenland.

By 1000 CE, Greenland was home to more than 300 farms on which people raised cattle or sheep or goats. They built many churches, including a huge cathedral. The ruins of the Gardar Cathedral can still be seen today.

Then

The Norse buried their hordes of silver to keep them safe. Sometimes they were unable to come back and claim them.

NOW

In 2013, two Danish teens found Viking treasure, including 60 rare coins.

Norse society lasted for 500 years on Greenland and then vanished. No one knows why. Perhaps it became so cold that farming was impossible. Maybe the settlers were attacked. It's a historical mystery that has never been solved.

Leif Erikson, one of Erik the Red's sons, also became an explorer. In 1000 CE, Leif heard stories of a new land from a sailor named Bjarni Herjolfsson and decided to sail there. He sailed west of Greenland all the way to North America!

DID YOU KNOW?

Leif's last name is Erikson because he was the son of Erik (Erik's son). If he had been a girl, her last name would have been Eriksdatter (Erik's daughter). That's how families used to form last names in Scandinavia.

Leif's crew came to the land of "Flat Stones," which archaeologists think might be Baffin Island, a large island off the coast of Canada. They sailed on to the "Land of Woods," thought to be Labrador, a region in northern Canada.

The third place they landed had grapes and streams full of salmon. Erik named this land Vinland, or Wineland. They stayed for one winter before returning home. Researchers believe Vinland was what is now a place in Canada called L'Anse aux Meadows.

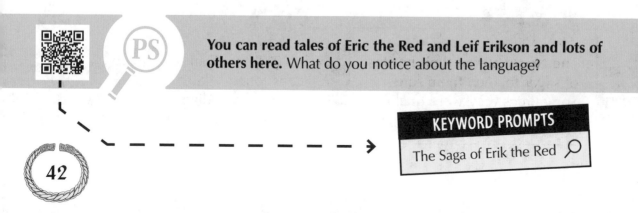

PS **You can read tales of Eric the Red and Leif Erikson and lots of others here.** What do you notice about the language?

KEYWORD PROMPTS

The Saga of Erik the Red 🔍

KNOW YOUR MYTHS

drinking horn: a horn used as a cup.

Words 2 Know

THOR AND THE GIANTS

One day, Thor, accompanied by Loki, went to Jotunheim to challenge the giants. The trip did not turn out as he thought it would. First, Thor failed at a drinking challenge, unable to drain his **drinking horn**. The giants gave him another task, to pick up a giant cat. Despite his best efforts, Thor could lift only a paw.

His last challenge was to wrestle a toothless old woman. Before Thor could refuse, she pinned him to the ground. Defeated, Thor returned to Asgard, where Loki explained the drink was really the sea, the cat was the world serpent, and the old lady was death. No one, not even a Norse god, can win against death.

THE SKRAELINGS

Sagas tell of Leif's brother, Thorvald, and another Icelandic explorer, Thorfinn Karlsefni, who tried to settle Vinland. There, they met Native Americans, whom they called the Skraelings. No one is certain what this word meant, but scholars think the word was not a very nice one. The Norse described these people as having large eyes and messy hair.

For a while, Native Americans traded fur pelts to the Norse for pieces of red cloth. During one trade, a Viking bull ran out of the forest, scaring the Native Americans away, but they later returned and attacked the Norse. In another saga, Freydis, the daughter of Erik the Red, frightened off a group of Native American attackers by holding her sword tightly to her chest.

The Norse were great explorers who traveled far across land and water before there were easy ways to travel. Of course, they weren't always welcome in these new lands. We'll see in the next chapter how they handled some of the problems of exploration.

? ESSENTIAL QUESTION

It's time to consider and discuss the Essential Question: How did geography play an important role in Viking history?

MEET THE GODS

LOKI

Loki was a mischievous god who enjoyed playing tricks on people. No one but him thought these jokes were funny. He cut off the hair of one goddess and kidnapped another. Sometimes, his tricks were cruel. One resulted in the death of a much-loved god. For this crime, Loki was punished.

Make Your Own Flatbread

**On ships, Vikings ate porridge, dried fish, and bread.
In this activity, you are going to make Viking bread.
Ask an adult to help you with the oven.**

SUPPLIES

* 1 cup barley flour or whole wheat flour
* 2 teaspoons flaxseeds
* pinch of salt
* large mixing bowl
* 3 teaspoons butter
* knife
* ⅓ cup water

1 Place all the dry ingredients into a large mixing bowl. Stir until mixed.

2 Chop the butter into tiny pieces and use your hands to mix in the butter. The mixture should feel like breadcrumbs.

3 Add the water and knead the dough until it comes together.

4 Cover the dough with a tea towel and let it rest for one hour. When the hour is almost up, preheat the oven to 300 degrees Fahrenheit (150 degrees Celsius).

5 Separate the dough into four balls. Flatten the balls to make small rounds.

6 Place the rounds onto a baking sheet and bake in the oven for 10–12 minutes.

45

VIKING GAME BOARD

The Norse faced many dangers as they traded and explored. In this game, you are on your first trading voyage to Constantinople. Will you make it to the fabled city?

SUPPLIES

* paper
* scissors
* pencil
* markers
* poster board
* glue
* 2 to 3 players
* coins for tokens
* die

1 Cut 20 circles out of paper. They must be large enough to write the different phrases on them.

2 In each circle write one of the following phrases.

- You are hired by a trading ship!
- Robbed on the way to the ship. Miss a turn.
- You remember to bring cloth, thread, and rope for ship repairs. Move ahead one space.
- Good winds. Roll again.
- Storm at sea. Miss a turn.
- Blown off course. Go back four spaces.
- Learn to navigate by the sun. Move your opponent's piece back two spaces.
- Design a weathervane.
- Stop in France, trade fish for wine. Roll again.
- Day of rest.

- You are a strong oarsman. Move ahead two spaces.
- Mend the ship's sail. Move ahead three spaces.
- You become seasick. Miss a turn.
- Make it to the Dnieper River!
- The crew must carry the ship around rapids. Miss a turn.
- Attacked by nomads. Go back three spaces.
- Good winds across the Black Sea.
- Make it to Constantinople. Roll again.
- Sell all of your furs for silver coins.
- Weak winds. Miss a turn.

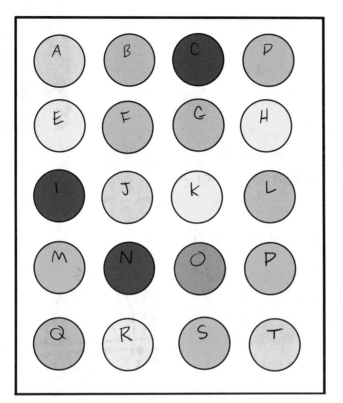

3 After filling in the circles, arrange them in a pattern in order on the poster board.

4 Glue down the circles, then decorate the rest of your game board.

To Play:

- Each player places a coin token on the first circle, "You are hired by a trading ship!" Players take turns rolling the die. The high roller goes first.

- Player #1 rolls the die and moves the correct number of spaces. Follow the instructions on the circle. If there are no instructions to move, the player remains on the circle until his or her next turn. The next player takes their turn.

- To win, a player must land directly on the last circle.

ACTIVITY

Make a Viking Lucet

Vikings used a knitting needle called a lucet to make cords and clothing.

SUPPLIES

- cardboard
- fork
- pencil
- scissors
- yarn

1 Trace the outside edge of a fork on the cardboard. You do not have to trace the individual prongs.

2 Cut out the fork. At the top, cut out a deep U.

3 Cut out or poke a small circle in the middle of the handle.

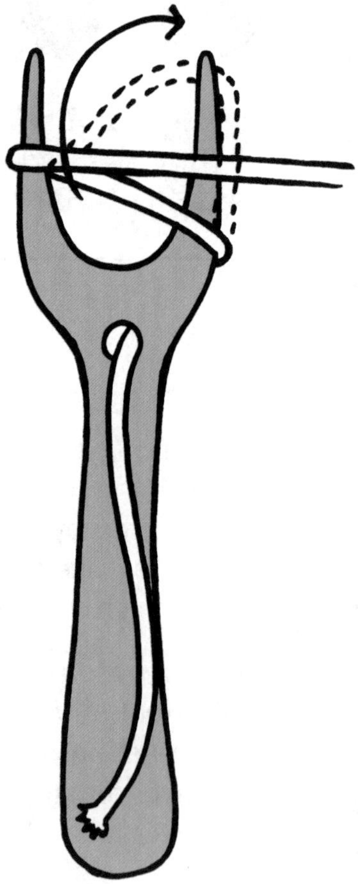

4 Thread the yarn through the middle from the back of the lucet to the front. Leave a good 4–6 inch tail. Hold the tail down with your thumb.

5 Wind the yarn counterclockwise around the right prong, clockwise around the left prong, and then back around the right prong. Repeat this three times so you have two figure eights.

6 Lift the bottom stitch over the top stitch on the right prong. Repeat this for the left prong. You have finished one stitch. Tighten by pulling gently on the tail.

7 Repeat steps four to six until your cord is the desired length.

8 To take your work off the lucet, leave a long tail, then run the cord in and out of the stitches, so your work does not unravel. Knot the end.

THINK MORE: What kind of clothing can you make with your cord? Draw some clothing designs in your study journal. How much cord will you need to make?

IS THIS VINLAND?

Up until the 1960s, historians were not sure where Vinland was or if it even existed. After all, Icelanders did not record the tales until centuries after the actual events. However, this didn't stop explorers Helge and Anne Stine Ingstad, who went in search of Vinland in Newfoundland, Canada. A fisherman led them to L'Anse aux Meadows (Meadow Cove), where they found evidence of a Norse settlement!

Several buildings, including a blacksmith shop, were unearthed. More than 2,000 eleventh-century Viking objects have been found since, including planks from a small boat, knitting tools, and a bronze pin Norsemen would have used to fasten their cloaks.

Today, the area is run by Parks Canada, which has rebuilt the Viking village. **You can see pictures of the rebuilt Viking settlement.**

KEYWORD PROMPTS

L'Anse aux Meadows National Historic Site 🔍

NORSE TRADING SCALE

Viking traders used a balance scale to weigh goods. Some could be folded, which made it easier for merchants when traveling. You'll make a simple scale out of an egg carton.

1 Cut off one long side from the egg carton lid. This will be the top of your scale. Poke a hole at either end of this strip and one in the center.

2 Join five paper clips together to make a chain. Hang this chain from one end of the strip. Repeat this step for the other side.

3 Cut out two, single egg containers. Make four more chains of four paper clips each. Attach two chains to each single egg container, one on each side.

4 Bring the two chains together and hang from one of the longer chains hanging from the top of the scale.

5 Place two clips in the center hole of the long strip. Hook onto the back of a chair or a railing.

6 Use your scale to weigh different small items. How do you know that one item is heavier than another? Make a chart in your study journal to keep track of items that are more or less heavy than other items. Are heavier items also more valuable?

CHAPTER 4
FIERCE FIGHTERS

In the eighth century, reports began to circulate of Viking raiders stealing treasure. The first recorded Viking raid took place in 793, when a group of Vikings attacked the **monastery** of Lindisfarne, off the coast of Scotland.

Scholar Alcuin of York described the raid in a letter. He wrote that the Vikings chased some of the **monks** into the sea, where they drowned. Others were taken away as slaves and church treasures were stolen!

? ESSENTIAL QUESTION

Why were the Vikings known for being fierce and terrifying raiders?

Words 2 Know

monastery: a place where monks devote their lives to prayer and religious study.

monk: a man who lives in a religious community and devotes himself to prayer.

51

A monastery might seem a strange place to attack, but the Vikings were pagans, not Christian. They did not think monasteries were special places. Monasteries had riches and were easy to raid because they weren't defended.

Villages along the coasts and inland waterways in Europe learned to fear the sight of a longship. A common prayer was, "From the fury of the Northmen, O Lord deliver us."

WHO WERE THE VIKINGS?

Viking society was divided into three main groups. At the top were jarls, who were rich landowners, chieftains, and kings. Below that were karls. Most people belonged to this group, including women, farmers, merchants, craftsmen, and warriors. People in the lowest group, the thrall, were slaves with no rights.

KARL

JARL

THRALL

From the time they were young, Viking boys learned the skills that would help them become warriors. They learned to hunt and played rough sports, such as wrestling. Lifting stones was a popular way to test a young man's strength.

VIKING RAIDS

The first Viking raids were small. Some were led by vicious men with scary names such as Sigurd Snake in the Eye or Eric Bloodaxe, who murdered his brothers to become king.

Later, Scandinavian kings, such as Sweyn Forkbeard and his son, Cnut the Great, began taking over large areas using thousands of men. These raids turned into permanent settlements. In 1016, Cnut became the first Viking king of England. During his reign, Denmark and some areas of Norway became part of his empire.

Vikings were so good at fighting that governments bribed them with silver to leave. This didn't work very well, though, because Vikings would come back for more.

Some people built **fortified** bridges to defend rivers from raids. But fortifications didn't stop Vikings from sailing hundreds of ships up the Seine in Paris in 885 CE! This is how a Viking ruler named Rollo was given land in France in 911 CE.

DID YOU KNOW?

Vikings in France were called Northmen. Can you see why Rollo's land came to be called Normandy?

WORDS 2 KNOW

fortified: strengthened with walls and trenches.

53

◇◇◇◇◇◇◇◇◇◇ NORSE WEAPONS ◇◇◇◇◇◇◇◇◇◇

In Norse society, where strength and fighting were valued, weapons were very important. Norse gods had many magical weapons. For example, Odin's spear never missed its target. Thor used magical iron gloves each time he threw his hammer. His magical belt, a gift from a giantess, made him even stronger.

KNOW YOUR MYTHS

SIGURD AND FAFNIR, THE DRAGON SAGA

Long ago, a greedy dwarf called Fafnir killed his father for treasure. Fafnir feared that someone else might take the treasure, so he transformed himself into a fire-breathing dragon. Fafnir's brother, Regin, waited until the time was right to steal the treasure.

Regin became the tutor to orphaned Prince Sigurd. When Sigurd grew up, Regin convinced him to set out on a quest for the treasure. He forged a magical sword named Gram for Sigurd from the broken pieces of his father's sword.

Sigurd succeeded in killing the dragon by piercing its heart with the sword. After tasting the dragon's blood, Sigurd became mightier and able to understand birds. The birds alerted Sigurd to Regin's plan to kill him and keep the treasure. Quickly, Sigurd pulled out his sword and killed Regin.

People could only dream of having weapons like the gods. Men charged into battle with a round wooden shield in one hand and a prized sword, battle-ax, or spear in the other. For extra protection, they wore a pendant around their necks shaped like Thor's hammer. This was believed to bring the wearer luck.

Weapons were signs of a warrior's status. Wealthy Vikings had swords beautifully inlaid with patterns of silver or copper. Some swords were even thought to have special powers. Their owners gave these swords impressive names such as "Leg-Biter." Swords were so valuable that a man might be buried with his or he might pass it down to his son.

CLEVER DWARFS

People who work with metal are called **smiths**, and they were highly regarded in Norse society. Smiths guarded the secrets of their **forges**. They only passed their knowledge down to sons or **apprentices**, which added to the mystery. Stories told that dwarfs used magic in their forges to create objects of beauty and wonder. Two of the cleverest of these craftsmen were Sindri and Brok.

Words 2 Know

smith: a person who works with metal.

forge: a place where metal is hammered into shape.

apprentice: a person who works with a master to learn a skill or trade.

55

Once upon a time, Loki bet them his head that they couldn't make objects equal to Dvalin's arts. Remember, Dvalin was the dwarf who made Sif's hair shine brighter than the sun. The two dwarfs accepted the challenge.

Loki never played fair. He turned into a pesky fly to distract them. The dwarfs pressed on to make a golden boar so bright it could turn night into day. They made a ring that produced more gold rings and a hammer that could crush mountains.

DID YOU KNOW?

Berserkers were a group of feared Viking warriors who worked themselves into a rage before a fight. Berserkers believed that they didn't need armor because Odin gave them special powers to protect them in battle. The modern word *berserk* comes from the Old Norse word *berserkr*.

Even though Loki lost the bet, he didn't lose his head. The dwarfs couldn't figure out how to take it without his neck. Instead, they sewed Loki's mouth shut!

THE END OF THE WORLD

One of the most often told myths was about a great battle. The Norse told the tale of Ragnarok as a story about the end of the world. Have you heard stories from today about the end of the world? Why is this an interesting subject for people to think about?

Vikings believed Odin sent his Valkyries to choose the most courageous of the dead to come with them to Valhalla, Odin's hall for the bravest men. Glittering spears lined the walls of Valhalla and gold shields formed its roof.

During the day, these warriors fought each other in preparation for Odin's final battle, Ragnarok. At night, Valkyries served the warriors food and drink and their wounds magically healed. You can read the myth about Ragnarok below.

?

ESSENTIAL QUESTION

It's time to consider and discuss the Essential Question: Why were the Vikings known for being fierce and terrifying raiders?

KNOW YOUR MYTHS

RAGNAROK: THE LAST BATTLE

For three long years, summer does not come. Then one day, people watch as the wolves Skoll and Hati devour the sun and the moon. The world shakes with such violence that stars fall to Earth. Loki, who is chained to rocks as a punishment for his role in another god's death, breaks free, as does the wolf Fenrir. From the depths of the ocean, the world serpent slithers onto the land. More enemies of Asgard, including frost giants, trolls, Hel, and the fire giant Surtur join to destroy the gods. The end is near.

Heimdall's horn sounds across Asgard. The gods and heroes of Valhalla charge. The air is thick with fire and smoke. Wolf Fenrir pounces upon Odin. Loki and Heimdall fight to the death. Though Thor defeats the world serpent, its venom kills him. With all the gods gone, Surtur waves his sword and sets the nine worlds on fire.

Out of the terrible destruction, a new world rises. A man and woman who had taken shelter by the world tree live. Baldr, the god of light, and his blind brother, Hoder, are born again. Peace and goodness rule once more.

FORTIFY A BRIDGE

King Charles II of France instructed his people to build barriers across the Seine River. He hoped that the Vikings would not be able to sail the blocked river to Paris. In this activity, decide how to defend your river.

1 In the cookie tray, spread out your sand. Create the course your river will take. Include at least one S-shaped curve. Create the banks of your river or other features, such as hills, by using more sand or soil, as well as landscaping items.

2 In the river, build your toothpick obstacles.

3 Next, using a little momentum, roll your marble toward the obstacles.

4 What happens? Were you able to construct a barrier that was strong enough to block the marbles?

5 Try to replicate a fast-flowing river by propping up your baking sheet with a book at one end. Your marble will roll more rapidly. Does this change your results?

THINK MORE: Try using other items as barriers. Which of your barriers worked the best and why? Would your results be different if you designed a different course for your river? Why?

SUPPLIES
* cardboard
* pencil
* scissors
* tempera paint
* paintbrush
* tinfoil
* glue
* yarn
* masking tape

MAKE A SHIELD

Different civilizations used different types of shields. Vikings used circular shields made from thin wooden planks. The middle of the shield had an iron dome to protect the shield bearer's hand. Another type of shield is the kite shield, which is wider at the top and pointier toward the bottom. You might have seen a knight of the Middle Ages using one of these! Which one provides more protection?

1 Trace around a pizza pan or similar object on the cardboard. Cut the circle out. Paint one side and let dry.

2 Cut out a small circle from the metallic paper for the middle of your shield. Cut tinier circles for the metal studs. Glue them in place.

3 For the handle, cut out two ruler-length pieces of yarn. Secure these on the back with tape.

4 Now make a kite shield with a rounded, upside-down triangle shape.

5 Which one covers more of you? Which one protects your body and legs? How can you improve the design?

Then

Norse warriors recycled the weapons they took from battles. York, England, contains an eleventh-century metalworking site where axes and sword parts were melted down to make new objects.

NOW

Scandinavians are leading the way in recycling. The country of Sweden sends only 4 percent of its trash to landfills.

MAKE AN OLD VIKING GAME

King's Table, or Hnefatafl, was a favorite Viking game in which players learned strategy. The rules for play are listed below. Two players are required.

SUPPLIES

✴ crafting felt
✴ pencil
✴ ruler
✴ permanent marker
✴ bowl 10 inches across
✴ scissors
✴ yarn
✴ coins, pebbles, or beads

1 Draw a 6-by-6-inch square in the middle of the felt.

2 Use the pencil and ruler to create a game board with nine rows across and nine rows down. Trace over the lines with a marker.

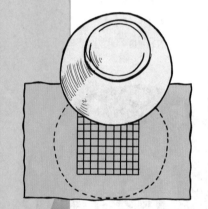

3 To make the pouch, put the bowl on the game board so it completely covers it. The center of the bowl should be above the center of the game board. Trace around the bowl and cut it out.

4 Use the point of the scissors to cut out evenly spaced holes around the edge. The holes should be roughly 2 inches apart.

5 Thread the yarn in and out of the holes. When not in use, tie the ends together to form a pouch to carry the game pieces.

6 Collect 24 games pieces, such as coins. You will need one for the king (quarter), 16 attackers (pennies), and 8 defenders (nickels).

Board Setup

- Put the king in the center.
- Place the king's defenders around this piece.
- Arrange the attackers in groups of four on all sides of the board.

Object of the Game

- The attackers try to trap the king. They can trap the king in a corner or box him in. Once the king cannot move, the attackers win.

Game Rules

- The king can stay in the center square. Other pieces can only move through it.
- The king can capture pieces.
- Pieces can only move in straight lines.
- Pieces can move as many squares as you like.
- Pieces are eliminated when boxed in.
- The attackers move first.

MEET THE GODS

Freya

Freya was the goddess of love and beauty who wore a beautiful gold necklace made for her by the dwarfs. She rode in a chariot pulled by cats. Flying over battlefields, Freya looked for warriors to join her in her palace in Asgard.

DESIGN A VIKING HELMET

Vikings did not wear helmets with horns. Real Viking helmets were plain and shaped to a person's head. A piece came down over the nose to protect it. Do you ear a helmet when you ride a bike or skateboard? What's different about your helmet?

SUPPLIES

✷ string
✷ paper bag
✷ scissors
✷ clear tape
✷ paper plate
✷ pipe cleaners
✷ scissors
✷ crayons, markers, pencil crayons
✷ stickers, glitter

1 Have a friend measure the circumference of your head with string. Now, cut a paper strip the same length. It needs to be 3 inches wide and rest comfortably above your ears. Secure the ends with tape.

2 Get some design ideas for your Viking helmet from your bike helmet. Begin adding elements to your helmet. Ask yourself these questions.

- How will your helmet protect your eyes, nose, ears, and mouth?

- How will you be able to see your enemy safely?

- How will your helmet make the enemy fear you?

3 When everyone has finished constructing their helmets, gather in one place. Choose one person to be the customer. Take turns explaining why the customer should buy your helmet. After a decision is made, choose another person to be the customer until everyone has had a turn.

CHAPTER 5
LASTING LEGACY

CHOMP
CHOMP
CHOMP

ZZ

What do you think future generations will know about your culture 1,000 years from now? The Viking Age lasted fewer than 300 years, but Norse gods such as Thor, Odin, Sif, and Loki still entertain people in movies. They are part of operas, video games, and novels. We get many of our ideas of bravery, battle, and fairness from the Norse myths.

The Norse also influenced the English language. For example, four days of the week are named for the Norse gods. Tuesday is for Tyr's day. Wednesday is for Wodin's day—Wodin was Odin's name in German. Thursday is for Thor's day and Friday is for Frigg's day.

? ESSENTIAL QUESTION

What contributions did Vikings make that affect the world today?

About 400 Norse words are part of the English language, including *anger*, *happy*, and *cake*. This is because the Norse controlled a large portion of England for more than 100 years.

One group of words greatly influenced by the Norse are place names. The word *by* is a Norse word for village or farmstead. Place names ending in *by* show that Vikings were there, such as Coleby or Tuthby in England. On the islands of Shetland and Orkney in Scotland, 99 percent of place names are of Scandinavian origin!

◇◇◇◇◇◇◇◇ VIKING TRADITIONS TODAY ◇◇◇◇◇◇◇◇

Vikings celebrated a holiday called Yule in mid-January with gifts, food, and drink. They sacrificed a boar to Frey in hopes of a good harvest and burned a large log called a Yule log. After the Vikings became Christian, this celebration grew into Christmas. Today, Yule logs are usually made of cake or chocolate and they are eaten instead of burned!

Even the custom of hanging mistletoe is from the Norse. In one myth, Frigg, the goddess of love and beauty, is afraid that her favorite son, Baldr, will die. She asks every living thing to promise never to hurt him. All agree, but Frigg forgets to ask mistletoe.

Loki learns of this. He tricks Baldr's blind brother, Hoder, into throwing a mistletoe spear at Baldr, which kills him. Baldr comes back to life after the battle of the end of the world.

Then

In 1828, a Swedish chemist named a new radioactive element Thorium after Thor.

NOW

Thor is a character in Marvel Comics' blockbuster movies starring Chris Hemsworth.

GOVERNMENT

Vikings settled disputes, made laws, and punished criminals at open-air meetings called Things. Each area had a Thing, but Vikings in Iceland had one for the entire island. In 938 CE, they established a parliament for all free people called the Althing. Once a year, free men came to talk.

The two-week meeting attracted people from across Iceland. It was a big social event where news was exchanged and marriages were arranged.

DID YOU KNOW?

Norse poets used phrases called *kennings* to describe people or objects without naming them. A bed of fish meant the sea. A wind racer was a horse. The word *kenning* comes from the Old Norse word *kenna*, meaning "to know."

Today, Iceland's democratically elected parliament is called the Althing. It is the oldest running parliament in the world.

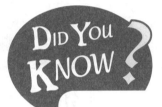

65

◇◇◇◇◇◇◇◇◇ *ART, MUSIC, AND LITERATURE* ◇◇◇◇◇◇◇◇◇

In the eighteenth century, Norse sagas became popular again. Writers such as James Macpherson, a Scottish poet, wrote poems with mythical heroes. This sparked a surge of interest in these stories.

Other writers followed him, including Danish poet Johannes Ewald, whose works featured Norse gods. Artists such as Nicolai Abildgaard and Henry Fuseli took subjects from Icelandic sagas, including Baldr's death and Thor battling the world serpent.

KNOW YOUR MYTHS

TALE OF BRUNHILDE

Brunhilde was a Valkyrie until she disobeyed Odin. As punishment, Odin put her into an everlasting sleep surrounded by a wall of fire. Only a truly brave man could free her. This man was Prince Sigurd. He slayed the dragon Fafnir and then learned about Brunhilde. He took the dragon's treasure, including a cursed gold ring. Not knowing that the ring would bring bad luck to anyone who wore it, Sigurd put it on.

Sigurd rushed to the castle where Brunhilde lay and plunged through the flames and saved her. She awoke at his touch. Sigurd had to leave, but he promised to return and marry her. Tragically, Sigurd drank a magic potion that made him forget all about Brunhilde. When he was later killed, Brunhilde joined him in death, where they could be together forever.

DID YOU KNOW?

Since 1951, Thor has been a character in Marvel Comics. Marvel has also made two movies featuring Thor (*Thor*, 2011, and *Thor: The Dark World*, 2013).

One of the best-known artists who incorporated Norse mythology into his work was nineteenth-century German composer Richard Wagner. Wagner's opera *The Ring Cycle* tells of the dwarf Alberich, who forges a magical ring that gives him unlimited power. Wagner added horns to Viking helmets to make the costumes more dramatic.

In the story, Wotan, King of the Gods, steals the ring, but it is soon snatched from him by two giants, Fafner and Fasolt. Next, the hero Siegfried (Prince Sigurd) sets out to retrieve the ring and finds the beautiful Brunhilde. You can read her myth on the opposite page.

POP CULTURE

The author J.R.R. Tolkien was a professor of medieval studies at the University of Oxford in England. He liked to tell his children stories about an odd creature called Bilbo Baggins, who found a cursed ring. This story became part of Tolkien's books. *The Hobbit* and *The Lord of the Rings* were inspired by Norse magic, dwarfs, and dragons. Even the names of the dwarfs who accompany Bilbo on his journey are from the *Eddas*, including Gandalf and Dvalin. Later, Tolkien's books were made into movies.

anime: Japanese animation.

manga: a term for Japanese-style comics.

runes: an ancient Scandinavian alphabet carved into stones or wood.

Words 2 Know

More recently, authors such as Neil Gaiman, Cressida Cowell, and J.K. Rowling have incorporated Norse myths into their works. Gaiman's *Sandman* graphic novels feature Norse characters such as Thor and Loki. Cowell writes about a Viking named Hiccup and his trained dragon. Rowling's *Harry Potter* books contain many references to Norse myths, such as Harry's invisibility cloak.

Anime and manga also portray Norse heroes. Myung-Jin Lee is the creator of *Ragnarok*. In the series, the Norse gods have sent Valkyries to stop the final battle before it begins.

KNOW YOUR MYTHS

ODIN AND THE RUNES

One day, Odin traveled to Yggdrasil for wisdom. He secured himself to the tree's great trunk with his sword. For nine days and nine nights, Odin went without food or drink. As the tree thrashed in the wind, Odin began to notice that the falling twigs formed symbols. This is how Odin learned to speak to the dead, protect those in battle, and calm the seas.

Odin used his spear to carve magical **runes** on plants and animals. He traced one onto the god Bragi's tongue to make him the god of poetry and song. Then, Odin traveled to Middle Earth and shared the secret of the runes with the wisest people there.

◇◇◇◇◇◇◇ MODERN TECHNOLOGY ◇◇◇◇◇◇◇

The Norse alphabet was called runes. It consisted of a system of straight lines. People carved the symbols of the alphabet onto stone, metal, wood, and bone. One of the most famous runestones is that of King Harald Blataud. He ruled Denmark and Norway. Rune stones with his initials have been found in Jelling, Denmark.

Have you ever seen a Bluetooth symbol on a cell phone? The translation for Blataud is "blue-tooth." The Scandinavian creators of Bluetooth remembered that King Blataud was known for bringing people together. Bluetooth brings different devices together. The Bluetooth symbol uses King Blataud's initials written in runes.

MEET THE GODS

HEIMDALL

Heimdall stands watch by the Bifrost Bridge, guarding the entrance to Asgard. He is armed with a sword and a long horn. When gods hear the sound of his horn, they know the end of the world, Ragnarok, is near.

? ESSENTIAL QUESTION

It's time to consider and discuss the Essential Question: What contributions did Vikings make that affect the world today?

CARVE A RUNE STONE

People chiseled runes into stone to mark important events. You can carve your own.

SUPPLIES

* ½ cup salt
* 1 cup flour
* large mixing bowl
* spoon
* ½ cup water
* baking sheet
* parchment paper
* paper clip
* pencil
* paper

1 Mix the salt and flour together. Slowly add the water. Knead the dough with your hands until it comes together, adding a little extra flour or water as needed.

2 Place a piece of parchment paper on a baking sheet. Mold a piece of dough into a rectangle on the parchment paper. Make the edges uneven so it looks like a worn rock.

3 Around the outside, draw a Norse-inspired design with a paper clip. In the center, write your message. The message can be about a special occasion, such as a birthday or the first day of school.

4 If you want your rune stone to stand up, position it with a lump of dough behind it. Let your dough harden overnight.

5 You can make rune stones to mark other important occasions. Perhaps it will become a Norse-influenced tradition for you?

SEND A MESSAGE WITH RUNES

By the end of the Viking Age, people used runes to send messages, such as "Come home." You and a friend can send secret messages to each other using runes.

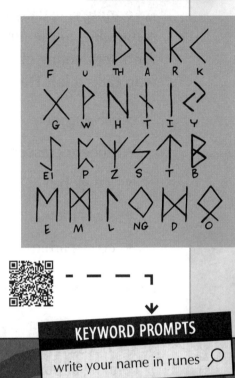

1 Write a short message. With an adult's permission, use this online rune translation tool to translate your message into runes.

2 Give the message to your friend. Can he or she figure it out? See if you can figure out your friend's response.

KEYWORD PROMPTS

write your name in runes 🔍

VIKING DISCOVERIES

In 1939, archaeologist Basil Brown made an amazing discovery at Sutton Hoo, England. He found a burial chamber under a large mound. It contained silverware from Byzantine, a beautifully carved helmet, and a sword with a snake-like pattern. Though the grave contained many objects, the identity of the person buried there is still a mystery. He may have been a high-ranking warrior or a king.

PS **You can see pictures of objects found at Sutton Hoo, which are kept at the British Museum.**

KEYWORD PROMPTS

excavations at Sutton Hoo 🔍

SUPPLIES

❋ pencil
❋ any object
❋ paper

CREATE YOUR OWN KENNING

A kenning is usually a two-word phrase that describes something. Some modern examples include "ankle biter" for a very young child and "motor mouth" for someone who talks a lot. Here are some kennings for the moon:

- silver sphere
- cheese crescent
- icy globe
- star's friend
- cold marble

Let's think of some of your own kennings.

1 Choose an object to write a kenning about.

2 Think about words that could represent this object. Make two lists of words that describe your object.

3 Choose a word from your second list and pair it with a word from your first. You can join the words together. Add adjectives or hyphens or change some of the words to make the phrases stronger.

THINK MORE: Can you think of other kennings that people use today? Why do you think people use kennings instead of the actual words?

MAKE A MISTLETOE WREATH

Legend says that after a mistletoe spear killed Frigg's son Baldr, she made the mistletoe promise to be used only for happiness in the future. Perhaps this is how kissing under the mistletoe became linked to the plant's goodness! Now, you can make a mini-mistletoe wreath.

1 Trace around the bowl on the cardboard. Place the cup in the center of the circle and trace around it.

2 Cut out the larger circle first. Then cut out the middle.

3 Cut out tear drop leaf shapes from the green paper. Glue them in place around the wreath.

4 Glue a few cotton balls on for berries.

5 Loop the ribbon around the top of your wreath and hang.

THINK MORE: Legends are always changing and evolving. Some historians think that Frigg was so sad that her son had died from mistletoe that she promised the plant would never again be used as a weapon. With an adult's permission, research other mistletoe myths online and in books. Based on your findings, write your own version of the legend.

CHAPTER 6
SIMILAR STORIES

For thousands of years, people have told myths and legends. Some stories are scary, while others are funny. They might be full of action or make you want to cry. Myths and legends tell of great heroes and nasty villains. Some describe real people and actual events.

Many of the stories from around the world have similar characters and themes. These include symbols such as rainbows, popular characters such as giants, and creation myths that explain how the world came to be.

? ESSENTIAL QUESTION

Why might you find similarities in myths from different areas?

RAINBOW MYTHS

Many cultures have myths that feature rainbows. Sometimes, a rainbow in a myth is a sign from the gods. In the Christian religion, there is a story in the Bible in which God shows Noah a rainbow. The rainbow represents God's promise never to send another flood to destroy the world.

Often, rainbows are paths from one world to another. In Japanese myth, a bridge of many colors hangs between heaven and the sea, just as the Norse bridge connects Asgard to Middle Earth. The Greeks also saw the rainbow as a path. Iris, the goddess of the rainbow, uses it to refill the clouds with rain from the sea.

Other cultures saw the rainbow as a living creature. The Maori of New Zealand believed that the rainbow is the god Uenuku. He was a man who transformed into a rainbow after he died.

GIANT MYTHS

Giants in myths have the power to create the world and destroy it. Sometimes giants act like bullies!

Then

The story of Beowulf, written around 700 CE by an English author, tells the tale of a Swedish hero who sets out to slay a monster named Grendel in Denmark.

NOW

In 2007, the animated action film *Beowulf* debuted on the big screen with the hero, his friend Wiglaf, and a group of soldiers traveling to Denmark to kill the monster Grendel.

Tales from Britain speak of giants hoarding treasure, living in caves, and harassing the local peasants. The Greeks imagined a race of giants whose parents were Gaia, the Earth, and Uranus, the sky. Hercules, the half-human son of Zeus, used thunderbolts and arrows to defeat them.

In Ireland, the giant Finn McCool built a causeway across the water so that he could challenge his rival, Benandonner. When Finn took a look at Benandonner, he realized that his rival was much larger than him. Finn's wife, Oonagh, then disguised him as a baby.

When Benandonner saw Finn the child, he was horrified because he thought that the child's father must be massive. He ran back to Scotland and tore up the causeway.

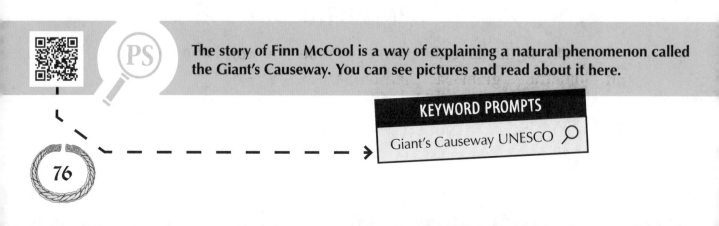

PS The story of Finn McCool is a way of explaining a natural phenomenon called the Giant's Causeway. You can see pictures and read about it here.

KEYWORD PROMPTS

Giant's Causeway UNESCO

KNOW YOUR MYTHS

ASGARD'S GIANT BUILDER

The Aesir and Vanir gods had ended their war with their two houses coming together. But the wall that once guarded Asgard lay in ruins. The gods' palaces and great halls lay exposed to the frost giants.

A mason happened to wander by and offered his services to the gods. The man, who was a giant in disguise, claimed that he could build a wall in less than three winters. For payment, he demanded Freya as his wife. Under Loki's suggestion, the gods agreed to the man's terms only if he built their wall in one winter.

The man agreed and went to work. His strong horse carried huge loads of rocks day and night. The wall took shape until it was higher than an iceberg and stronger than steel. The gods worried that the man might complete the wall in time. They didn't want Freya to leave Asgard, so Loki came up with a devious plan.

While the man worked on the wall, a mare appeared and lured his horse away. Without it, the man could not finish the wall. He flew into a rage and exposed his real giant self to the gods. In the spring, a **foal** appeared in Asgard with eight legs. Odin named the horse Sleipnir. It was faster than the wind and able to race over land and water.

Words 2 Know

foal: a horse that is less than one year old.

77

✧✧✧✧✧✧✧✧✧✧ FANTASTIC BEASTS ✧✧✧✧✧✧✧✧✧

Practically every ancient culture imagined incredible beasts. They might have heads of one animal and tails of another. Some were destructive fire breathers with equally bad tempers. Others were wise and helped create the world.

The Greeks believed a terrifying monster lurked in a cave by the sea. Skylla was 12 feet long and waited hungrily for unsuspecting ships to pass by. It would rear one of its six heads, flash its rows of teeth, and devour the ship whole!

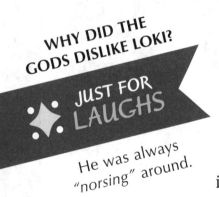

WHY DID THE GODS DISLIKE LOKI?

JUST FOR LAUGHS

He was always "norsing" around.

China has a tale of four good dragons. These dragons saw that people were dying because the rains had not come. So they scooped up seawater and poured it upon the farmers' fields. The Emperor of Heaven became angry at the dragons and buried them under mountains. He did not want the dragons to end the **drought**. That power belonged to the Emperor of Heaven.

Words 2 Know

drought: a long period of time when it doesn't rain as much as usual.

THE CREATION MYTHS

Creation myths tell how everything was made. In Norse myth, the sons of Bor, Odin, Hoenir, and Lothur were out walking when they found two logs. Grasping hold of the logs, they ripped them from the ground. One log became the first man, Ask. The other log became the first woman, Embla. The gods gave Ask and Embla souls, understanding, and five senses.

Hinduism explained that all life came from Lord Brahma. When he got lonely, Lord Brahma created people, plants, and animals from his body. In one story, the god of destruction, Vishnu, destroyed his work each night. Lord Brahma recreated life each day.

The Native American Blackfeet tell of Napi, who was curious about a world covered in water. He sent a duck, an otter, and a badger to investigate, but they were unable to tell him anything. Finally, Napi sent a muskrat, who brought back a lump of clay. Napi blew upon the clay, transforming it into Earth. He molded more clay into people and taught them how to live.

The dragons were able to escape. They transformed themselves into the four great rivers of China, so the people never had to go without water again.

◇◇◇◇◇◇◇ FOODS OF EVERLASTING LIFE ◇◇◇◇◇◇◇

Many cultures spoke of mythical food and drink that helped their gods stay young. Greek and Roman gods drank nectar called ambrosia. Stories say it flowed through their veins instead of blood.

DID YOU KNOW?

The Norse divided their gods into the Aesir and the Vanir. Some scholars believe that the groups stood for two large classes within Norse society. The Aesir represented Norse warriors, and the Vanir represented the peasants.

In Hindu mythology, the gods and the demons were forced to work together in order to churn the nectar of immortality out of the Ocean of Milk. They used the serpent, Vasuki, as a rope. They wrapped Vasuki around the golden mountain, Mandara, and started churning. For thousands of years, they churned the ocean until only the Nectar of Immortality was left.

The Chinese tell a story about the Monkey King, who was invited to heaven by the Jade Emperor. He was asked to guard the Garden of the Immortal Peaches. Each peach took 6,000 years to grow. Whoever was lucky enough to eat a peach would live forever. The Monkey King wanted a peach so badly that he didn't just eat one but all of them!

Myths from around the world show us what life was like in ancient times. We read them to discover what people found important and how they explained the world. What stories do we tell about ourselves that you think will survive 1,000 years or more into the future?

? ESSENTIAL QUESTION

It's time to consider and discuss the Essential Question: Why might you find similarities in myths from different areas?

SUPPLIES

* paper
* pencil
* pencil crayons
* markers
* ruler

NORSE GODS COMIC STRIP

The Norse gods went on many adventures. You can plan an exciting new journey for your own Norse characters!

1 Write your story. It will need a beginning, middle, and an end. Your story can be about heroes or villains, or maybe it explains something, such as thunder.

2 Section another piece of paper into 8–10 boxes. Draw each important scene from your story into the boxes. Include speech bubbles and color.

3 Share your comic with a friend.

MEET THE GODS

FREY

Frey was the god of the sky, rain, and harvest. He was Freya's twin. Frey ruled over the light elves. He was originally a Vanir god, but came to live with the Aesir after the gods' war. Frey had a magical ship and a golden boar named Gullinbursti.

ACTIVITY

SUPPLIES

* Internet access
* study journal
* pencil

COMPARE AND CONTRAST RAINBOW MYTHS

In this book, you read about the rainbow in Norse mythology. With an adult's permission, go online or to a library and research a rainbow myth from another culture, such as the Ojibwe Nation or the ancient Greeks. Alternately, you may choose a different mythological symbol or theme mentioned in this chapter. Consider the similarities and differences between the two mythologies and write a short essay about them.

1 Write three sentences about how the events in the myths are similar, different, or both.

2 Write three sentences about how the central ideas in the myths are similar, different, or both.

3 What are the characters' unique strengths and weaknesses?

4 Do either of the mythologies have any relationship to the truth of how rainbows are made? You can research the science behind the creation of rainbows and view some pictures here.

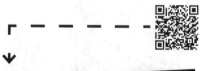

KEYWORD PROMPTS

rainbow National Geographic

82

MAKE A NORSE MONSTER

There are some very strange monsters in Norse myths. In this activity, you can create your own.

1 Before you begin, think about what makes your creature unique. Where do you think it lives? What does it eat? What does it want most of all? What special powers does it have?

2 Cut out a piece of paper to fit the container.

3 Use your pencil crayons to create a design on this paper and glue to the container.

4 Use the supplies you have gathered to create arms, legs, or eyes. Attach these with glue. Be creative!

SUPPLIES

* ✳ small yogurt container, empty and clean
* ✳ paper
* ✳ scissors
* ✳ pencil crayons
* ✳ glitter
* ✳ white glue
* ✳ pipe cleaners, google eyes, buttons, scraps of paper, pinecones, yarn, etc.

NORSE ADVENTURE MADLIB

Use the parts of speech and as many glossary words as you can to fill in the blanks and complete this silly story!

* **noun:** a person, place, or thing.
* **plural noun:** more than one person, place, or thing.
* **adjective:** describes a noun.
* **verb:** an action word.
* **adverb:** a word that describes a verb. Many adverbs end in -ly.

During the month of _____ (MONTH), I traveled to Asgard with _____ (NORSE GOD NAME). We rode _____ (ADVERB) over the rainbow bridge in our _____ (NOUN) pulled by _____ (PLURAL NOUN). At the bridge we were stopped by _____ (NORSE GOD NAME). He was _____ (VERB) his _____ (NOUN).

Suddenly, _____ (NUMBER) trolls appeared and _____ (VERB PAST TENSE) over the bridge. They were armed with _____ (PLURAL NOUN) and _____ (PLURAL NOUN). I had never seen trolls before. Their skin was covered in _____ (NOUN) and they made a terrible _____ (NOUN) as they _____ (VERB PAST TENSE). I was horrified, but _____ (NORSE GOD NAME) and I did not run. I decided to _____ (VERB) after the trolls.

They ran straight into Iduna's _____ (NOUN) where she was busy picking _____ (NOUN) for the gods. The trolls began to _____ (VERB) all the _____ (PLURAL NOUN). Iduna chased them with a _____ (NOUN). I grabbed a _____ (NOUN) and began chasing after them too. Before long, nearly all the gods of Asgard were _____ (VERB ENDING WITH "ING").

The trolls could not escape. So, they _____ (VERB) into Odin's _____ (NOUN) where _____ (NUMBER) men had been invited to a _____ (NOUN). When the trolls saw the _____ (NOUN), they stumbled back _____ (VERB ENDING WITH "ING"). Just then, the _____ (ADJECTIVE) _____ (NOUN) (name of Norse god) appeared and the trolls raced back over the rainbow bridge.

I followed them with _____ (NORSE GOD NAME) down to _____ (NOUN), where we entered a _____ (ADJECTIVE) _____ (NOUN). It was very dark and _____ (ADJECTIVE). Before _____ (NORSE GOD NAME) could _____ (VERB), we _____ (VERB) the stolen apples and decided to _____ (VERB) to Asgard. I can't wait to have another _____ (NOUN), but I don't want to see trolls ever again!

anime: Japanese animation.

apprentice: a person who works with a master to learn a skill or trade.

archaeologist: a person who studies ancient people through the objects they left behind.

artifact: an ancient, man-made object.

aurora borealis: a natural display of shimmering colors in the night sky, usually only seen in the far north. Also called the northern lights.

ballast: weight in the bottom of a ship that helps to balance the ship.

berserker: a ferocious, uncontrollable fighter.

boar: a large, pig-like animal.

bow: the front of a ship.

bracteate: a thin metal disc with an engraved image that could be worn around the neck.

British Isles: England, Scotland, Wales, all of Ireland, and 5,000 small islands.

Byzantine Empire: also called Eastern Roman Empire, founded by Constantine the Great in 330 CE.

cargo: a load carried on a ship or aircraft.

CE: put after a date, CE stands for Common Era and counts up from zero. BCE stands for Before Common Era and counts down to zero. These non-religious terms correspond to BC and AD. This book was published in 2015 CE.

chain mail: a type of armor worn by warriors made of interlocking metal links.

crops: plants grown for food and other uses.

culture: a group of people who share beliefs and a way of life.

drinking horn: a horn used as a cup.

drought: a long period of time when it doesn't rain as much as usual.

fates: powers that are believed to control what happens in the future.

fjord: a long, narrow inlet of the sea, usually with steep cliffs on both sides.

foal: a horse that is less than one year old.

forge: a place where metal is hammered into shape.

fortified: strengthened with walls and trenches.

glacier: a huge mass of ice and snow.

hull: the hollow, lowest part of a ship.

latitude: imaginary lines around the earth that measure a position on the earth to the north or south of the equator.

legend: a story about heroes from the past.

livestock: animals raised for food and other uses.

longboat: a large boat powered by oars.

manga: a term for Japanese-style comics.

mead: an alcoholic drink made with honey and water.

medieval: the period of European history between the fall of the Roman Empire and the Renaissance, from about 350 to about 1450.

Midsummer: a holiday celebrating the longest day of the year.

mineral: a naturally occurring solid found in rocks and in the ground. Rocks are made of minerals. Gold and diamonds are precious minerals.

monastery: a place where monks devote their lives to prayer and religious study.

monk: a man who lives in a religious community and devotes himself to prayer.

myth: a traditional story that expresses the beliefs and values of a group of people.

mythology: a collection of stories that are often focused on historical events. Myths express the beliefs and values of a group of people.

natural phenomenon: an event, such as a thunderstorm or an earthquake, that is created by nature, not by people.

navigate: to find your way from one place to another.

Norse: the people of ancient Norway, Sweden, Denmark, and Iceland.

Norse myths: ancient stories from northern Europe.

Old English: a language spoken in England between the fifth and eleventh centuries.

Old Norse: a language spoken during the Viking Age.

pagan: a person who worships many gods.

runes: an ancient Scandinavian alphabet carved into stones or wood.

sacrifice: an animal, plant, or a person that is offered to the gods.

saga: a long poem.

skald: a professional Norse poet.

smith: a person who works with metal.

soapstone: a type of soft stone that can absorb and give off heat.

stern: the back of a ship.

supernatural: beings, objects, or events that cannot be explained.

tide: the daily rise and fall of the ocean's water level near a shore.

topographical: having to do with the features of the land, such as mountains.

tribe: a large group of people with the same language, customs, and beliefs.

Valkyries: warrior goddesses who carried slain warriors to Odin's hall.

Vikings: people from Scandinavia who raided coastal towns in Europe between the eighth and tenth centuries.

whetstone: a stone used for sharpening knives or tools.

METRIC CONVERSIONS

Use this chart to find the metric equivalents to the English measurements in this book. If you need to know a half measurement, divide by two. If you need to know twice the measurement, multiply by two. How do you find a quarter measurement? How do you find three times the measurement?

English	Metric
1 inch	2.5 centimeters
1 foot	30.5 centimeters
1 yard	0.9 meter
1 mile	1.6 kilometers
1 pound	0.5 kilogram
1 teaspoon	5 milliliters
1 tablespoon	15 milliliters
1 cup	237 milliliters

BOOKS

Ceceri, Kathy. *World Myths and Legends*, Nomad Press, 2010

D'Aulaire, Ingri, and d'Aulaire, Edgar Parin. D'Aulaires' *Book of Norse Myths*, NYR Children's Collection, 2005

Hoena, Blake. *National Geographic Kids Everything Mythology: Begin Your Quest for Facts, Photos, and Fun Fit for Gods and Goddesses*, National Geographic Children's Books, 2014

Woolf, Alex. *Meet the Vikings (Encounters with the Past)*, Gareth Stevens Publishing, 2014

Ganeri, Anita. *The Vikings (All About Ancient Peoples)*, Stargazer Books, 2010

Davis, Graeme. *Thor: The Viking God of Thunder (Myths and Legends)*, Osprey Publishing, 2013

McCullough, Joseph. *Dragonslayers: From Beowulf to St. George (Myths and Legends)*, Osprey Publishing, 2013

Denton, Shannon Eric. *Thor: Short Tales: Norse Myths*, Magic Wagon, 2010

Colum, Padraic. *The Children of Odin: The Book of Northern Myths*, Aladdin, 2004

Osborne, Mary Pope. *Favorite Norse Myths*, Scholastic, 2000

WEBSITES

NOVA: pbs.org/wgbh/nova/vikings

Jorvik Viking Centre: Great Britain:
jorvik-viking-centre.co.uk

The Norse in the North Atlantic:
heritage.nf.ca/exploration/norse.html

History of the Nordic Region: norden.org/en/
fakta-om-norden-1/history-of-the-nordic-region

BBC History:
bbc.co.uk/schools/primaryhistory/vikings

Story Nory-Norse Myths:
storynory.com/category/myths/norse

Vikings Training School Game:
nms.ac.uk/explore/play/discover-the-vikings/
vikings-training-school

QR CODE INDEX

Page 4: merriam-webster.com

Page 6: en.wikipedia.org/wiki/
Temple_at_Uppsala#mediaviewer/File:
Olaus_Magnus_-_On_the_Glorious_Temple_
Devoted_to_the_Nordic_Gods.jpg

Page 8: gutenberg.org/files/18947/
18947-h/18947-h.htm

Page 15: bbc.co.uk/history/ancient/vikings/
religion_01.shtml

Page 30: irisharchaeology.ie/2012/09/the
-oseberg-viking-ship-burial

Page 34: appcrawlr.com/ios/star-chart

Page 40: bl.uk/learning/timeline/item126532.html
• britannia.com/history/docs/asintro2.html

Page 42: sagadb.org/eiriks_saga_rauda.en

Page 49: whc.unesco.org/en/list/4/gallery

Page 71: pbs.org/wgbh/nova/ancient/write-your-
name-in-runes.html • britishmuseum.org/explore/
highlights/relationships.aspx?page=34602&Title=
Excavations+at+Sutton+Hoo&ContentType=
Article&PageId=23432&relationtypestoshow=
highlight%20objects

Page 76: whc.unesco.org/en/list/369

Page 82: education.nationalgeographic.com/
encyclopedia/rainbow

ESSENTIAL QUESTIONS

Introduction: Do you think the Vikings had a choice in how they behaved?

Chapter 1: Why did the Norse explain their world through myths?

Chapter 2: Why were the Vikings excellent shipbuilders?

Chapter 3: How did geography play an important role in Viking history?

Chapter 4: Why were the Vikings known for being fierce and terrifying raiders?

Chapter 5: What contributions did Vikings make that affect the world today?

Chapter 6: Why might you find similarities in myths from different areas?